JOAB:
KING DAVID'S
TOP GENERAL

ESSENTIAL LESSONS ON CHARACTER

To Daniel Silliman,

It takes a lot to write about
difficult topics. That requires
grit and a strong character. You
embody both.

ADEYINKA ADEGBENLE

2/16/21

JOAB: King David's Top General
Essential Lessons on Character

Copyright © 2020 by Adeyinka Adegbenle

ISBNs:
978-1-7362207-0-2 (paperback)
978-17-362207-1-9 (eBook)

Published by Ways of Excellence LLC

CONTENTS

PREFACE

JOAB HAD IT ALL. Power, prestige, wealth and fame. He also happened to be very good at his job as the commanding general of the Nation of Israel's army. Joab was world class! A thoroughbred one might even add. He was a magnificent and courageous warrior on the battlefield. He served his master and nation well, with a record of not losing a single battle during his 40-plus years as head of the army and second in command to King David.

He was also a master political strategist. In this book, I aim to help you—the reader, get to know the man—Joab. Not just to know him, but to learn from how he lived his life—both his triumphs and his tragedies—and apply those lessons to better your life. The accounts detailed in this book are from the 120-plus verses where Joab is mentioned in the Bible: The Old Testament sections of The New International Reader's Version, or NIRV, specifically.

Joab played a major role in the history of Israelites, especially during the reign of David. He took command of the army and won several major victories for the Kingdom of Israel.

I hope the lessons from the story of Joab help you to grow in excellence on your journey toward becoming an even better version of yourself. I hope you get to see in Joab's life story that there are several non-debatable character qualities that every person should possess, irrespective of how good or talented he/she is.

Happy reading,
Adeyinka Adegbenle.

CHAPTER 1

THE STORY OF JOAB is part of a bigger one concerning a nation: Israel, chosen by God himself. The Israelites had been in captivity in Egypt for 430 years. Through several mighty miraculous acts—the 10 plagues, detailed in Exodus 7–12, God delivered them from the hands of their oppressors and slave masters.

God then entered into a mutual covenant relationship based on love with this nation that he had chosen to be his own. The covenant called for the freed Israelites to abide by the terms of the agreement: They must be faithful to God and obey his laws. Doing so would ensure peace, prosperity and many other benefits for them and their descendants.

You are a holy nation. The LORD your God has set you apart for himself. He has chosen you to be his special treasure. He chose you out of all the nations on the face of the earth to be his people.

The LORD chose you because he loved you very much. He didn't choose you because you had more people than other nations. In fact, you had the smallest number of all. The LORD chose you

3

because he loved you. He wanted to keep the promise he had made to your people of long ago. That's why he used his mighty hand to bring you out of Egypt. He bought you back from the land where you were slaves. He set you free from the power of Pharaoh, the king of Egypt. So I want you to realize that the LORD your God is God. He is the faithful God. He keeps his covenant for all time to come. He keeps it with those who love him and obey his commandments. He shows them his love.

— Deuteronomy 7:6-9

The terms of the covenant with Israel are summarized in the Ten Commandments:

I am the LORD your God. I brought you out of Egypt. That is the land where you were slaves.

Do not put any other gods in place of me.

Do not make for yourself statues of gods that look like anything in the sky. They may not look like anything on the earth or in the waters either. Do not bow down to them or worship them. I, the LORD your God, am a jealous God. I cause the sins of the parents to affect their children. I will cause the sins of those who hate me to affect even their grandchildren and great-grandchildren. But for all time to come I show love to all those who love me and keep my commandments.

Do not misuse the name of the LORD your God. The LORD will find guilty anyone who misuses his name.

Remember to keep the Sabbath day holy. Do all your work in six days. But the seventh day is a sabbath to honor the LORD your God. Do not do any work on that day. The same command applies to your sons and daughters, your male and female servants, and your animals. It also applies to any outsiders who live in your towns. In six days the LORD made the heavens, the earth, the sea and everything in them. But he rested on the seventh day. So the LORD blessed the Sabbath day and made it holy.

Honor your father and mother. Then you will live a long time in the land the LORD your God is giving you.

Do not murder.

Do not commit adultery.

Do not steal.

Do not be a false witness against your neighbor.

Do not want to have anything your neighbor owns.

Do not want to have your neighbor's house, wife, male or female servant, ox or donkey.

— Exodus 20:1-17

Just like the laws of nature, the benefits and consequences of abiding by the given laws were pre-built into the covenant.

Despite all the blessings God offered them, the Israelites were not consistently loyal to him. Thus commencing cycles where the Israelites obeyed God for short periods of time. Doing so released the inherent blessings and benefits that the nation would enjoy, with great prosperity, peace and protection from all enemies. Then after a while, they would become complacent and half hearted in abiding by the terms of the covenant and drift toward breaking the terms. That led to unleashing the built-in negative consequences—defeat by enemy nations, famine, and being exiled to lands of their enemies, to name a few.

As time went on during the bad periods, they would cry out to God for help. Out of mercy and love for his chosen nation, God would respond positively. Help came in the form of leaders (judges and prophets) that God used to deliver the Israelites from their oppressors and restore peace to the land.

Once delivered out of the hands of their oppressors, and with peace restored, the Israelites would again forget all about their God and the covenant, repeating the cycle yet again.

We meet Joab at the point of the story of the Israelites where they had recently transitioned to a political system headed by King Saul, from the former system where God ruled over them via prophets and judges. But Saul failed miserably, and God was forced to look for a replacement. That replacement came in the person of David.

David was secretly anointed as the next king of Israel by the prophet Samuel at a very young age, not given exactly in the Bible. Biblical scholars believe it to be about fifteen. Saul was still the sitting king of Israel at the time.

The Lord said to Samuel "How long will you be filled with sorrow because of Saul? I have refused to have him as king over Israel. Fill your animal horn with olive oil and go on your way. I am sending you to Jesse in Bethlehem. I have chosen one of his sons to be king."

But Samuel said, "How can I go? Suppose Saul hears about it. Then he'll kill me."

The LORD said, "Take a young cow with you. Tell the elders of Bethlehem, 'I've come to offer a sacrifice to the LORD.' Invite Jesse to the sacrifice. Then I will show you what to do. You must anoint for me the one I point out to you."

Samuel did what the LORD said. He arrived at Bethlehem. The elders of the town met him. They were trembling with fear. They asked, "Have you come in peace?"

Samuel replied, "Yes, I've come in peace. I've come to offer a sacrifice to the LORD. Set yourselves apart to him and come to the sacrifice with me." Then he set Jesse and his sons apart to the LORD. He invited them to the sacrifice.

When they arrived, Samuel saw Eliab. He thought, "This has to be the one the LORD wants me to anoint for him."

But the LORD said to Samuel, "Do not consider how handsome or tall he is. I have not chosen him. The LORD does not look at the things people look at. People look at the outside of a person. But the LORD looks at what is in the heart."

Then Jesse called for Abinadab. He had him walk in front of Samuel. But Samuel said, "The LORD hasn't chosen him either." Then Jesse had Shammah walk by. But Samuel said, "The LORD hasn't chosen him either." Jesse had seven of his sons walk in front of Samuel. But Samuel said to him, "The LORD hasn't chosen any of them." So he asked Jesse, "Are these the only sons you have?"

"No," Jesse answered. "My youngest son is taking care of the sheep."

Samuel said, "Send for him. We won't sit down to eat until he arrives."

So Jesse sent for his son and had him brought in. His skin was tanned. He looked very healthy. He had a fine appearance and handsome features.

Then the LORD said, "Get up and anoint him. This is the one."

So Samuel got the animal horn that was filled with olive oil. He anointed David in front of his brothers. From that day on, the Spirit of the LORD came on David with power. Samuel went back to Ramah.

— 1 Samuel 16:1-13

Saul knew he had been rejected by God as king, but he did not know who the next king would be. Over time, through a series of events though, he suspected it was indeed David. This led to an uncontrollable jealousy of David and an incessant pursuit to kill him.

The full narration of these events can be found in 1 Samuel and 2 Samuel.

David, who became a highly skilled and successful warrior and a leading commander in Saul's army, was now forced to flee for his life from his king and master. His only crime was that Saul suspected he was going to usurp him as the next king of Israel, and Saul was not going to let that happen under his watch.

ESSENTIAL LESSON

The path to seeing one's dreams accomplished is not linear. In fact, far from it. Just ask any successful person you know. The path is marked with many highs and lows.

David faced a lot of challenges after he was anointed as the next king of Israel. He felt discouraged at times, but he never gave up on his calling, and of course he did eventually become a mighty king. We all go through challenging times in life. However, challenging times only last but for a season.

CHAPTER 2

WHILE ON THE RUN, David was forced to hide in caves and even in cities of the enemies of the Israelites.

> *David left Gath and escaped to the cave of Adullam. His brothers and the other members of his family heard about it. So they went down to join him there. Everyone who was in trouble or owed money or was unhappy gathered around him. He became their commander. About 400 men were with him."*
>
> *— 1 Samuel 22:1-2*

Among those who joined him while on the run were Joab and his two brothers. At this very point of the story, in 1 Samuel 26, David learns that Saul and his men are again close on his heels. He gathers intelligence to ascertain where Saul and his men have set up camp. Once he gets this information, David decides to go and see the situation firsthand to prepare and plan should war break out. David saw Saul sleeping in the camp. His army commander, Abner, son of Ner, was also lying close by and keeping watch over his king. The rest of the army, three thousand elite warriors, were camped all around Saul, protecting him. These were no ordinary conscripts who had nothing else to do. They were highly skilled, fully trained and ready for battle at the drop of a hat. 1 Samuel 26:2 explains it this way:

> *So Saul went down to the Desert of Ziph. He took 3,000 of the best soldiers in Israel with him. They went to the desert to look for David.*

After David scopes out the enemy's camp, for reasons best known to him, he decides to go right into their midst. It is at this moment that we are introduced to Joab, via his brother Abishai. This is the first time Joab's name is mentioned in the Bible:

> *Then David spoke to Ahimelek, the Hittite.* **_He also spoke to Joab's brother Abishai, the son of Zeruiah._** *He asked them, "Who will go down with me into the camp to Saul?"*
> *"I'll go with you," said Abishai.*
> — *1 Samuel 26:6*

In the passage above, do you see what just transpired? Ahimelek I'm sure hesitated going into the enemy's camp. He probably thought to himself, "These guys are after us to KILL US. We should be running far away from them in the opposite direction and not going down into their camp. We would literally be giving ourselves over to the enemy. Has David lost his sense of reasoning?"

David asked both Ahimelek and Abishai, brother of Joab the same question: "Who will go with me into the camp of Saul?" Notice how Abishai jumped at the chance almost before the words were completely out of David's mouth? Talk about being FEARLESS! BOLD! and COURAGEOUS! Abishai was one of David's most skilled warriors and leaders. Yet, the author of 1 Samuel deliberately introduced Abishai as "Joab's brother," as if to give us a peek into what was to come. I can imagine the author saying: "Oh! And that's only the brother. Wait till you meet the man Joab himself."

ESSENTIAL LESSON

When confronted with a choice of being brave or giving in to fear, choose to be brave. After this particular incident, there is no mention of Ahimelek the Hittite again in the Bible. Abishai, however, went on to become a great leader in David's army when David became king (he led a division of twenty-four thousand soldiers).

CHAPTER 3

THE GENEALOGY OF JOAB'S family is given in 1 Chronicles 2:13-16.
Jesse's first son was Eliab. His second son was Abinadab.
The third was Shimea. The fourth was Nethanel.
The fifth was Raddai. The sixth was Ozem.
And the seventh was David.
Their sisters were Zeruiah and Abigail.
Zeruiah's three sons were Abishai, Joab and Asahel.

Joab is the middle son. His mother, Zeruiah, is the older of David's two sisters. The other sister is Abigail. Some scholars believe that Zeruiah's mother was initially married to the Ammonite King Nahash and gave birth to Zeruiah and Abigail with him before she married David's father, Jesse. The passage in 2 Samuel 17:25 alludes to that:

Amasa was the son of a man named Jether, an Israelite who had married Abigail, the daughter of Nahash and sister of Zeruiah the mother of Joab.

So Joab was David's step-nephew. They were not related by blood, contrary to popular belief.

Most biblical characters are listed or introduced based on their male ancestors. For example: David the son of Jesse and Saul the son of Kish. Zeruiah's sons are an exception, as they are mentioned throughout the Bible with the matronymic "Sons of Zeruiah," suggesting that she was a woman of great importance, most likely because she was the daughter of King Nahash of Ammon.

Abishai, who agreed to go with David into the enemy's camp, was Joab's older brother. All three were highly regarded soldiers and leaders in David's large army once he became king.

Asahel, the youngest, served as a commander of twenty-four thousand men. Asahel was well known for being very swift on his feet; some said he ran like a gazelle.

Asahel's son Zebadiah also led a troop of twenty-four thousand men in King David's army. Abishai, the oldest, was the commander over David's "Three Mighty Warriors" described in 2 Samuel 23:18. He also was a very senior army commander. He is credited with killing an astonishing eighteen thousand men of Edom in the Valley of Salt, says 1 Chronicles 18:12

The name of their father is not mentioned in the Bible, only that he was deceased and buried in Bethlehem.

They took Asahel and buried him in his father's tomb at Bethlehem.

— 2 Samuel 2:32

He may have died while his three boys were very young. This could be another reason why Joab and his two brothers were better known and referred to as the "sons of Zeruiah."

Joab, as we can see, was from a family of high achievers. All of his brothers were high-ranking successful individuals and outstanding warriors. They were all endowed with great talents. Only the very best made it into the king's army. They did not just make the cut as grunts, but were top officers. In ancient times, serving the king was a dream job for many. Serving as a leading official in the king's army spoke volumes about the individual, much less to have all members of one family in distinguished positions of great authority. Such families were revered in ancient days. Joab's family was one of a kind.

ESSENTIAL LESSON

Every human being is endowed with a special talent: It's that thing that you do easily and better than most people. Your talent is God's gift to you. Identify your talent, develop it to its full potential and use it in every way possible. You will be well on your way to fulfilling your life's purpose. You can support yourself and achieve great success with your talent. Joab and his brothers recognized and developed their talents very early on in life, and they courageously embraced and pursued them. They all ended up becoming very senior leaders in one of the most prestigious armies of their time.

CHAPTER 4

SAUL DID EVENTUALLY DIE in battle against the Philistines:

The Philistines fought against the Israelites. The Israelites ran away from them. But many Israelites were killed on Mount Gilboa. The Philistines kept chasing Saul and his sons. They killed his sons Jonathan, Abinadab and Malki-Shua. The fighting was heavy around Saul. Men who were armed with bows and arrows caught up with him. They shot their arrows at him and wounded him badly.

Saul spoke to the man carrying his armor. He said, "Pull out your sword. Stick it through me. If you don't, these fellows who aren't circumcised will come. They'll stick their swords through me and hurt me badly."

But the man was terrified. He wouldn't do it. So Saul took his own sword and fell on it. The man saw that Saul was dead. So he fell on his own sword and died with him. Saul and his three sons died together that same day. The man who carried his armor also died with them that day. So did all of Saul's men.

The Israelites who lived along the valley saw that their army had run away. So did those who lived across the Jordan River. They saw that Saul and his sons were dead. So they left their towns and ran away. Then the Philistines came and made their homes in them.

— *1 Samuel 31:1-7*

Shortly after Saul died, David moved to Hebron, a town in the Kingdom of Judah. He moved there with his men and family.

They made their homes in Hebron and other nearby towns.

Then the men of Judah came to Hebron. There they anointed David to be king over the people of Judah.

— *2 Samuel 2:4*

David did not immediately become king over the whole of Israel at this point. He was anointed king over a smaller part of Israel: Judah this second time. He ruled as king of Judah for seven and a half years.

Saul's army commander, Abner, who survived the war against the Philistines, had brought Saul's son Ish-Bosheth to Mahanaim in Israel and made him king over the other, larger territories of Israel.

Well, the newly installed King David was not just sitting around. There was plenty of enemy territory to conquer.

First on the list was Jebus, better known as Jerusalem. David decided that this was going to be the capital of his kingdom. Jerusalem is positioned right in the middle of the Israelite territory. The only problem was that Jerusalem was a highly fortified Canaanite city. No other enemy kingdom had succeeded in conquering this city. The Jebusites, the dominant Canaanite tribe, were so confident in how impenetrable their city was that when David marched his army up the city's walls, they mocked him, saying in 2 Samuel 5:6:

"You will not get in here; even the blind and the lame can ward you off."
They were so presumptuous that some historical records mentioned that they truly manned the walls with the blind and lame.

David knew this was going to be a tough conquest. Ordinary tactics would not do any good in this situation. He had to think outside of the box. David had somehow discovered that the city of Jebus had a secret water system to bring water from outside into a local point in the city. He knew that this would be possibly the only way to get into this highly fortified city. Being the master strategist that he is, rather than charging up against the fortified city walls, he knew that the water shaft was the only way to get into the city and only one man could go up the shaft. Once the man succeeded in gaining entry into Jebus, he would then be able to let the rest of David's soldiers in via the main city gate.

This was a highly dangerous mission. Climbing up the shaft would be no easy feat. David came up with a plan. As incentive, he promised the position of the highly esteemed commanding army general/second in command to the king to the soldier who dared to lead the mission and succeed.

One man rises to the challenge—Joab. This was almost like a death sentence. Even Joab's older brother—the impetuous Abishai—did not dare take on this foolhardy mission. Or it could be that Joab beat his older brother to stepping out to volunteer.

Climbing up the water system was next to impossible because of how the water shaft was constructed. We know more about the water shaft system now, thanks to an archaeologist named Charles Warren, who discovered a shaft in 1869 that is believed to be the same one! The shaft is popularly known as Warren's Shaft, named after the man who discovered it.

Just to put things into perspective here: the city of Jebus was on a hill. In Joshua 11:3, the Jebusites were referred to as the people who "lived in the central hill country." Getting water into the city required a very sophisticated system. This system not only had to get water from down below upward to the hill country, it also must not make them vulnerable to the enemy. So it had to be hidden and well fortified.

Joab somehow managed to make his way up this complex water tunnel and into Jebus undetected and unharmed. He launched a surprise attack and was able to let the rest of the army in. David was then able to capture Jebus and make it the capital of his kingdom. David later on renamed the city Jerusalem.

Joab, by excelling at this very risky mission, did earn himself title of second in command to the most powerful and popular king at the time—David.

Now Joab was army commander, chief of staff and the king's right-hand man. Not so long ago he was just a soldier and now was the second most powerful man in the kingdom. His story and reputation, not all of it as glorious, only grow from there.

Once they captured Jerusalem, David rebuilt the city. His right-hand man is not just waiting around. He also works alongside his master to ensure the city is restored. I imagine the city sustained much damage from the battle between the Jebusites and David's men. This was going to be the king's place of abode after all. Their national capital, with a Capitol Hill. It had to be very secure and safe. It also had to be a city fit for a king—hence Joab's role in the restoration.

Joab again rose to the occasion. He wanted the position of army general so much that he was willing to risk his life by doing the impossible. It is very easy to say he had the foresight to know that David would eventually become king of the entire territory of Israel and thereby increase his own influence and power over time. So even though he was a commander now over just the four hundred men and soldiers from Judah, he knew it was only a matter of time before those numbers expanded to hundreds of thousands more, once David took his position over the remaining larger territories of Israel.

ESSENTIAL LESSON

High risk brings high rewards but, of course, the possibility of huge losses also. Joab knew very well that climbing up the water shaft would be a great, perhaps lethal, risk. But he wanted the sure promotion to army general badly enough that he was willing to take that risk. Yes, he could have failed, but he did not.

If you are ever faced with such a choice (but not life-threatening!), choose to take the risk. Whatever the outcome, you will at least know that you tried.

Be bold, and mighty forces will come to your aid. – Goethe

CHAPTER 5

IN AN ATTEMPT TO try to regain control over Judah, Abner, Saul's army commander, marched out with his army to Gibeon. Joab marched his army out to meet them. The commanders met at the pool in Gibeon. (A famous water landmark of the time.) One group sat down on one side of the pool, and the other group sat on the other side. That they both sat down implies this was a conference of sorts. Both groups, though enemies in the real sense, met to see the possibility of reaching an agreement to preclude a costly war.

Well things escalated quickly when Abner suggested that twelve men be counted off from each group to fight each other to determine which group was stronger or which would win. Both units of the twelve men chosen from Joab's army and Abner's army faced off and stabbed each other simultaneously and died. Then a war between the two armies broke out from there.

Before we move on any further, note that it was Abner who instigated this war. He came to meet Joab and his men at the pool of Gibeon. It was Abner who suggested that groups from each side fight. Joab was there to defend the Kingdom of David. Joab was there doing his job as army commander. But Joab should not have agreed to Abner's senseless request. He should have known better as the leader. After all, he was responsible for those under him.

The battle was heavy, Joab was there with the very best soldiers and that included his brothers, Abishai and Asahel. Abner and his men lost the battle. Asahel, as mentioned previously, was both a seasoned leader in the army and "as fast and swift as a gazelle." Asahel could run! Being light-footed and swift was a valued gift in ancient times.

During the course of battle, Asahel chased after Abner to kill him and hopefully end the fighting. Abner told Asahel several times to desist from chasing him because he knew who he was and of course he did not want to make an already bad situation worse by being the person who killed Joab's younger brother.

> *The three sons of Zeruiah were there. Their names were Joab, Abishai and Asahel. Asahel was as quick on his feet as a wild antelope. He chased Abner. He didn't turn to the right or the left as he chased him. Abner looked behind him. He asked, "Asahel, is that you?"*
>
> *"It is," he answered. Then Abner said to him, "Turn to the right or the left. Fight one of the young men. Take his weapons away from him." But Asahel wouldn't stop chasing him. Again Abner warned Asahel, "Stop chasing me! If you don't, I'll strike you down. Then how could I look your brother Joab in the face?"*
> *— 2 Samuel 2:17-22*

Asahel refused to listen, and Abner had no choice. If Asahel caught up to him, he would kill him. So Abner drove the end of the blunt end of his spear into Asahel.

I don't think he intended to kill Asahel, otherwise Abner would have used the sharp point of his spear. Sadly, Asahel died as the blunt end still came out through his back.

Asahel's failure to listen and reason with Abner after several warnings had just cost him his life. If only he had listened.

In 2 Samuel 2:23 it states: *Every man stopped when he came to the place where Asahel had fallen and died. But Joab and Abishai chased Abner.*

Why did the men stop? Because it was the right thing to do. Some who stopped were most likely members of the twenty-four thousand men under Asahel's command (1 Chronicles 27:7). A mighty leader and warrior had just fallen. Their leader was dead. Shock! Disbelief! They stopped out of respect and honor for this valiant and gifted warrior. They stopped because it is what most of us, if in their shoes, would do. To them this fight had gone a bit too far and it was time to call off this unwarranted, senseless fight.

Joab and older brother Abishai came upon the body, too. But they did not stop. Instead they chased Abner. Both remaining two brothers continued in their pursuit of Abner, intending to kill him, not to have a chit-chat. They had a job to do: Hunt and destroy the enemy. Grief and anything else must wait till after the battle was over.

Eventually the pursuit and fight were called off by Joab when Abner spoke out by saying Joab's men should desist from pursuing and killing their fellow Israelies.

> *Abner called out to Joab, "Do you want our swords to keep on killing us off? Don't you know that all this fighting will end in bitter feelings? How long will it be before you order your men to stop chasing their fellow Israelites?"*
>
> *Joab answered, "It's a good thing you spoke up. If you hadn't, the men would have kept on chasing them until morning. And that's just as sure as God is alive."*
>
> *So Joab blew a trumpet. All the troops stopped. They didn't chase Israel anymore. They didn't fight anymore either.*
>
> *— 2 Samuel 2:26-28*

Abner and the Israelites lost the battle to David's men. All in all, nineteen men had died from David's side, aside from Asahel, while Joab's army had killed three hundred and sixty men from the army Abner led.

The two armies then turned back and went back to their bases.

Despite this momentary truce, the warring between the Royal House of Saul and the Royal House of David continued for a long time. David's house grew stronger over time while Saul's house grew weaker.

ESSENTIAL LESSON

A lack of discernment–the ability to judge well, can lead to deadly consequences. Abner was an experienced and battle-hardened warrior. Asahel, even with his special talent of speed, was no match for Abner. Asahel's life was cut short abruptly because of personal poor judgment. He was stubbornly bent on having his own way. A wise person and leader knows when to be humble enough to listen to the voice of reason and also yield to better reason. If only Asahel had taken a moment to listen to Abner, he most likely would not have died on the battlefield on that day.

CHAPTER 6

A FEW YEARS AFTER David became king over Judah, it happened that Ish-Boseth: ruling king of the northern territories of Israel and the king of the majority, accused Abner of sleeping with one of his late father's concubines, Rizpah. A concubine is a mistress, who cohabits in the household with a married man and has sexual relations with him, however he never marries her. A side-chick of sorts. A common practice in Old Testament times.

Abner did not take this accusation lightly. King Ish-Boseth had just bitten the hand that feeds him. Lets not forget that it was Abner who went to get Ish-Boseth and made him king. Abner was the real power behind the throne. Ish-Boseth was just the puppet king.

This accusation of sinful behavior so deeply upset Abner that he told Ish-Boseth that he would now help David become the king of the whole of Israel.

Abner was very angry because of what Ish-Bosheth said. So Abner answered, "Do you think I'm only a dog's head? Am I on Judah's side? To this day I've been faithful to the royal house of your

*father Saul. I've been faithful to his family and friends. I haven't
handed you over to David. But now you claim that I've sinned
with this woman! I will do for David what the LORD promised
him. If I don't, may God punish me greatly. I'll take the kingdom
away from Saul's royal house. I'll set up the throne of David's
kingdom over Israel and Judah. He will rule from Dan all the
way to Beersheba." Ish-Bosheth didn't dare to say another word
to Abner. He was much too afraid of him.*

— 2 Samuel 3:8-11

Abner was true to his word. He sent word to David about his
intentions. Abner was a powerful and very influential man. He rallied
the elders of the land together and spoke to them about making David
king over the rest of Israel, just as God had promised.

He then sent a message to David saying:

*"Make a covenant with me. Then I'll help you bring all the
Israelites over to your side."*

— 2 Samuel 3:12

David agreed, Abner got the ball rolling, he succeeded in convincing all of the leaders of Israel to make David their king. He then
visited David with twenty of his top officials to finalize the details
and commence the succession of David as king of all Israel. David
welcomed Abner and his men with much pomp. He held a big feast
for them. They discussed all they needed to and then Abner and his
men left peacefully. All of this happened while Joab was away at war
defending the kingdom.

Soon after Abner's departure, Joab arrived from the war front. He
learned that Abner had just left, and that the king gave him a very nice
welcome and sent him on his way peacefully. Joab almost exploded
in anger. "You have got to be kidding me!" he must have thought.

In that full rage mode, he went to the king:

What have you done? Abner came to you. Why did you let him get away? Now he's gone! You know what Abner, the son of Ner, is like. He came to trick you. He wanted to watch your every move. He came to find out everything you are doing."
                                                    — *2 Samuel 3:24-25*

I can imagine him just not letting David get a word in, or David, seeing the rage of Joab, decided it would be best to keep quiet and talk to him later. Whatever David's thoughts were, he did not say anything to Joab.

It would not be too far-fetched to assume that part of the covenant Abner made with David would involve making Abner army commander in place of Joab. Abner was more experienced, more influential and had been army commander of Israel much longer than Joab. He knew Israel well. He was still very powerful. Let it not be lost on the reader, Abner had single handedly succeeded in convincing the leaders of Israel to go along with his plans of making David king over them.

Abner and David also went way back. He had introduced David to King Saul. That led to David becoming a senior official in Saul's army, before Saul turned on David out of jealousy. By the way, that introduction came after the famous biblical story of David and Goliath, the Philistine.

After David killed Goliath, he returned to the camp. Then Abner brought him to Saul. David was still carrying Goliath's head.
"Young man, whose son are you?" Saul asked him.
David said, "I'm the son of Jesse from Bethlehem."
                                                    — *1 Samuel 17:57-59*

Abner was an army commander decades before David became king. From a political and strategic perspective, it would be of great benefit to have Abner installed as King David's top general, over Joab. All in all, it would be hard to imagine Abner reporting to Joab. Insulting even, and I doubt Abner would have agreed to those terms. Maybe this was why David did not utter a word when Joab confronted him.

Keep in mind that Joab was oblivious to all that had actually transpired between David and Abner. He had been away fighting wars, so as far as he was concerned, the king had no business locking arms with Abner, who not only was a rival army commander, but also the man who had killed his brother Asahel. I'm also certain that he got full details about the real purpose behind Abner's visit.

Still in that full rage mode, Joab decided to handle matters himself. What happened next is a real tragedy.

ESSENTIAL LESSON

There is always more to the picture or story than meets the eye. Things aren't always what they seem. You should always be careful about jumping to hasty conclusions. Every story has two sides to it. Pause and Breathe. Listen to both sides before making a decision. It's just another good way to exercise wisdom.

CHAPTER 7

JOAB LEFT THE KING, he then sent messengers to Abner asking him to return to Hebron. Upon Abner's return, Joab slyly took him to a room under the pretense of wanting to discuss an important matter with him. Once Abner was in the room with Joab and his remaining brother, Abishai, Joab murdered Abner in cold blood by stabbing him in his stomach. As Abner's life slipped away, Joab must have felt that he both avenged his brother at last and also eliminated his most dangerous rival.

2 Samuel 3:30 says this:

Joab and his brother Abishai murdered Abner. They did it because
he had killed their brother Asahel in the battle at Gibeon.

Uncontrolled rage, coupled with unforgiveness, drove Joab to slay Abner.

There are many Bible verses about the dangers of not keeping anger in check, for example:

Foolish people let their anger run wild.
But wise people keep themselves under control.
— *Proverbs 29:11*

Those who control their anger have great understanding; those
with a hasty temper will make mistakes.
— *Proverbs 14:29*

An angry person stirs up fights.
And a person with a bad temper commits many sins.
— *Proverbs 29:22*

If only Joab had kept his cool and given some thought to what he was about to do. He most likely would not have committed premeditated murder. Or maybe Joab had been looking for the opportune time to take revenge on Abner for killing Asahel. Whatever the case, Joab, with the assistance of his older brother Abishai, had just murdered Abner. A mighty commander had fallen.

When David heard about what had happened, he was deeply hurt and let out a cry of sorrow as recorded in 2 Samuel 3:28:

I and the people of my kingdom aren't guilty of spilling the blood
of Abner, the son of Ner. We are free of blame forever in the
sight of the LORD.

I'm sure David at this point realized that he could easily meet the same fate as Abner at the hands of Joab if he did not tread carefully, so instead of challenging "raging Joab" directly, he pronounced curses on him and his lineage. Here is what he said:

May Joab and his whole family line be held accountable for spilling Abner's blood! May Joab's family never be without someone who has an open sore or skin disease. May his family never be without someone who has to use a crutch to walk. May his family never be without someone who gets killed by a sword. And may his family never be without someone who doesn't have enough to eat.

— 2 Samuel 3:29

I am pretty sure he uttered those curses in the absence of Joab and Abishai, who probably had not yet returned from where they met and killed Abner. Or Joab knew the king definitely would be deeply upset with his actions, and as a result decided to stay away from the palace at that moment.

King David was sad, angry and deeply upset at what just happened. David proclaimed his innocence in the presence of many. From the way he lamented and wept out loud over Abner's death, everyone in his Kingdom was truly convinced he had nothing to do with the murder.

Still, David, it seemed, was too scared of his army commander to confront him. Instead he ordered Joab and those with him to wear mourning clothes and march in front of Abner's corpse, while the king marched behind the bier. Abner was buried in Hebron, Judah.

King David sang a song of sadness over Abner. He said,

"Should Abner have died as sinful people do?
 His hands were not tied.
 His feet were not chained.
 He died as if he had been killed by evil people."

— 2 Samuel 3:32-34

The king out of fear must have chosen his words very carefully when he addressed his servants over the incident. He simply said:

> Don't you realize that a great commander has died in Israel today? I'm the anointed king. But today I'm weak. These sons of Zeruiah are too powerful for me. May the LORD pay back the one who killed Abner! May he pay him back for the evil thing he has done!
>
> — 2 Samuel 3:38-39

Verse 39 summed up King's David's feelings and anxieties about Joab and his brother:

"These sons of Zeruiah are too powerful for me."

If the elders had suspected David of playing a part in Abner's murder, it would have caused the king many serious problems. His chances of ever becoming king over the remaining regions of Israel would have ended right there and then. Abner's murder could have led to a full-blown war between the two regions, as northern Israel could have retaliated by attacking their fellow countrymen in the south. It could have turned into a real blood bath.

The effects of the impetuous and senseless murder of Abner by Joab and Abishai went beyond just appeasing their thirst for revenge of the death of their younger brother.

ESSENTIAL LESSON

Decisions you make when angry and emotionally charged, will nine times out of ten be decisions you regret. Whenever we make hasty decisions, we are bound to make mistakes. When tensions are high, that is exactly the time when you should not make any major decisions. Walk away from an emotionally charged situation to help you calm down and regain full control of your senses, if you need to. Not only that, but as a leader, the negative consequences of such decisions have compounded effects. Hundreds, thousands and even hundreds of thousands of others can be negatively impacted by just one wrong decision by a leader.

When a large tree falls in the forest, it does not always fall alone, it takes several others down with it. ~ African proverb

CHAPTER **8**

JOAB, IN THE SHORT time after David made him his army general, had proven to be a superb commander. So much so that David let him go off into battle without him. Joab grew in popularity and power as a result.

Shortly after the murder of Abner, King Ish-Boseth, ruler of the other major states of Israel, was murdered in his own kingdom. Now a huge part of Israel had no king. The kingless tribes of Israel all came to ask David to be their king.

> *Then all the tribes of Israel came to see David at Hebron. They said, "We are your own flesh and blood. In the past, Saul was our king. But you led Israel on their military campaigns. And the Lord said to you, 'You will be the shepherd over my people Israel. You will become their ruler.'"*
>
> *All the elders of Israel came to see King David at Hebron. There the king made a covenant with them in front of the Lord. They anointed David as king over Israel.*
>
> *David was 30 years old when he became king. He ruled for 40 years.*

— 2 Samuel 5:1-4

When David became king over all of Israel, Joab automatically also became the supreme commander of the joined nation's entire army. The number of men under him increased exponentially into the hundreds of thousands. His sphere of influence had just grown significantly. Now he was responsible for more men, and now greater power had now been bestowed upon Joab.

Life continued, and it was business as usual for the king and his army commander. Joab was busy protecting the kingdom and I'm sure settling into his new role commanding the huge army now under him. David was also busy in his new role as a king with much greater responsibilities.

It happened that Nahash, king of the Ammonites, died. When David got the news, he remembered the kindness that Nahash had shown him in the past. The Bible does not say what Nahash did, but he likely helped David when he was on the run from Saul. Also, let's not forget that Nahash was the father to David's step sisters, Zeruiah and Abigail. I'm sure they had known each other long before David became king.

David sent delegates to Ammon to express his condolences to the son of the late Nahash, Hanun, who is now the sitting king of Ammon. Things did not exactly go as planned. When David's envoys arrived, they spoke first with the commanders of the Ammonite army, who relayed their message to the new king. They said: "Well David has sent the delegates here to express his sadness over your father's death. That's an outright lie. We believe they have come to spy out the land to identify weak spots to help them plan their attack."

Keep in mind that during this time, Israel was an undefeated superpower. Under David's leadership, the nation had turned back to God and was enjoying years of prosperity and victory. So you can see why the Ammonites were scared and intimidated by the entourage of high-ranking officials sent by David.

When Hanun heard that, he ordered his guards to grab the delegates, and to disgrace and humiliate them by cutting off their clothes from the waist down and cutting off half of each man's beard. Then he sent them on their way back to Israel.

Let's put things in today's perspective. Imagine the president of the United States sends his secretary of state, the vice president and a few other top officials to one of our ally nations to express his condolences over the passing of their president. However, upon getting there, they are accused of being spies, roughly handled and humiliated by having their hair shaved off till bald, and cutting off their clothes and undergarments from the waist down. Then they are sent back to the United States, back to the president that way. Imagine seeing the senior officials of the president in that state all over the news. That was exactly what happened here.

Well, of course news got back to King David about what had happened. And of course he was furious. When the Ammonites realized they had angered David, they went and hired twenty-two thousand Aramean soldiers, they also hired the King of Maakah and one thousand men, and another twelve thousand men from Tob—all to help them fight against the powerful Israelites.

When David heard what they had done, he mobilized Joab and all of the fighting men in Israel to go out and fight the Ammonites.

Upon getting to the battlefield, Joab did not know that the Ammonites had hired neighboring armies as mercenaries to join them in combat. Joab saw that the battle lines of enemy soldiers were behind and in front of him. In other words, he was pinned in.

Watch how this strategic skilled army commander displays outstanding mastery of bravery in the face of fear and imminent danger.

So he chose some of the best troops in Israel. He sent them to march out against the Arameans. He put the rest of the men under the command of his brother Abishai. Joab sent them to march out against the Ammonites. He said, "Suppose the Arameans are too strong for me. Then you must come and help me. But suppose the Ammonites are too strong for you. Then I'll come and help you. Be strong. Let's be brave as we fight for our people and the cities of our God. The LORD will do what he thinks is best."

— 2 Samuel 10:9-12

The Ammonites and Aramean army ran away from Joab and Abishai once they saw they were under attack. They ran back into their cities. Joab and his men did not pursue them, and marched back to Jerusalem.

Upon the army's return, David learned that the Arameans had gone to find even more fighting men to help them as they regrouped and prepared to attack Israel. Upon hearing that, David himself mobilized Israel's army and led it out to face the Arameans in battle.

Joab did not go this time. The kingdom could not be left unprotected. So he remained with a contingent of his fighting men, who were probably tired and needed to recuperate from the earlier fighting against the Ammonites and Arameans.

David and his men defeated the Arameans. The Bible says David's forces killed seven hundred of their chariot riders, and forty thousand foot soldiers. He also struck down Shobak, the commander of their army.

The Arameans were bought under the rulership of the Israelites. After that, the Arameans were afraid to help the Ammonites again.

ESSENTIAL LESSON

Be careful of whom you receive advice from. The inexperienced King Hanun heeded to wrong counsel—which ended up costing him and his kingdom greatly, both in lives and legacy. A very costly war between Hanun's kingdom and Israel could have been prevented. You should always take the time to conduct your own due diligence, or even seek the advice of additional counsel before making a major decision.

CHAPTER 9

It was spring. It was the time when kings go off to war. So David sent Joab out with the king's special troops and the whole army of Israel. They destroyed the Ammonites. They marched to the city of Rabbah. They surrounded it and got ready to attack it. But David remained in Jerusalem.

— 2 Samuel 11:1

IN THE VERSE ABOVE, we see a now too-common pattern: David sending Joab off to fight his wars. Joab had shown himself to be an outstanding and dedicated general with superb military acumen. He easily held his own on the battlefront, even in the absence of the king. Despite his temperament, Joab repeatedly had proven that he was up to the task of leading his massive army to victory after victory.

Still, as the verse above clearly points out: During that time, kings were expected to be away at war, on the battlefield leading their army.

We are not told why David did not do as he was supposed to. All we know is that he was at the wrong place at the wrong time.

Joab, meanwhile, successfully attacked those still-troublesome Ammonites, and finished up the job he started in previous chapters. He then marched to Rabbah, their capital.

One night, David was bored and restless. Maybe because his mind kept drifting to the ongoing war with the Ammonites that he should have been leading. Keep in mind there were no phones back then to get instant updates on the ongoing war.

David got out of his bed and took a stroll on his rooftop. The rooftop of the king's palace was probably higher than those of the other houses. David had a clear view into the compounds of those who lived nearby. As he walked along the palace rooftop on this particular night, David spotted a beautiful lady taking her bath. She was naked. This king was already married to three women and had several more concubines. David did not look away. Instead he inquired about who she was from a messenger. The messenger confirmed that her name was Bathsheba and that she was married to Uriah, one of David's most elite soldiers. He was away on a campaign with Joab.

Well, David sent for Bathsheba and had a one-night stand with her. Not too long after that, Bathsheba sent a message to the king informing him that she was pregnant. The series of events that unfolded next never cease to leave me speechless every time I read about them in the Bible.

David sent a message to Joab, ordering Uriah's return. Upon Uriah's arrival, David asked him about Joab and the other soldiers and got updates about the war. He then told him to go home and spend some quality time with his wife, since he has been away on the battlefield for so long. Uriah left the palace but he did not go home. Instead he decided to spend the night by sleeping next to David's servants by the entrance of the palace. When David found this out, he was perplexed and asked Uriah why he did not go home to his wife. Uriah's reply, in 2 Samuel 11:11:

The ark and the army of Israel and Judah are out there in tents.
My commander Joab and your special troops are camped in the

open country. How could I go to my house to eat and drink?
How could I go there and sleep with my wife? I could never do
a thing like that. And that's just as sure as you are alive!

David then proceeded to put his Plan B into motion. He invited
Uriah to dinner that night, intentionally got him drunk and then told
him to go home to his wife. By having Uriah go home to sleep with his
wife, David hoped to pass off his impregnation of Bathsheba as Uriah's
doing. However this noble loyal servant and soldier still did not go home,
but spent the night again on a mat with the servants. When David found
out that he did not go home again that second night, he knew he could
do nothing to persuade Uriah to go home and sleep with his wife.

David proceeded to Plan C. He sent Uriah back to Joab with a
message. The message Uriah carried had his death sentence. Unknown
to Uriah, he departed from Jerusalem for the last time. He saw his
king and master, whom he had served faithfully for many years, for
the last time. Unknown to Uriah, he walked back to the battlefield
to fight his very last battle.

The letter David sent to Joab through Uriah bore these words:

Put Uriah out in front. That's where the fighting is the heaviest.
Then pull your men back from him. When you do, the Ammonites
will strike him down and kill him.

— 2 Samuel 11:15

The words in that letter are painful to read.

Joab knew his master well, he was also an extremely smart leader.
Bathsheba, Uriah's wife, and David were not the only two privy to
what happened the night David slept with her. The messenger who
was sent to go get Bathseba knew. The guards at the palace gate all saw
her being escorted into the king's private chambers. Just like today,
news like that traveled like wildfire and certainly Joab knew what

45

had happened between Bathsheba and David. He must have pressed the messenger whom David sent to get Uriah for more information about why Uriah was being singled out by the king, out of a hundred thousand plus soldiers on the field that day. Why Uriah?

Joab followed his king's orders.

After Joab murdered Abner, we do not hear of anything between Joab and his master again until the incident involving Bathsheba. All we know is David was deeply upset about that murder. It would not be too far-fetched to assume that Joab had been looking for ways to get back into his David's good graces. The role of acting as an accessory to the murder of Uriah and being the executioner of David's plan to murder to Uriah on the battlefield, provided the perfect opportunity for Joab. David also knew from past experience that there was no better person to flawlessly carry out his dirty work than the ruthless Joab.

Let it not be lost on us that this is the same David who cried a river of tears after Joab murdered Abner. The same David who wept and lamented loudly over Abner's demise, went to great lengths to orchestrate the murder of an innocent man, just to cover his own misdeeds. Birds of the same feather do indeed flock together!

So Joab attacked the city. He put Uriah at a place where he knew the strongest enemy fighters were. The troops came out of the city. They fought against Joab. Some of the men in David's army were killed. Uriah, the Hittite, also died.

— 2 Samuel 11:16-17

Joab sent a messenger back to the king with news about all that had happened in battle, including Uriah's death.

He told the messenger, "Tell the king everything that happened in the battle. When you are finished, his anger might explode. He might ask you, 'Why did you go so close to the city to fight against it? Didn't you know that the enemy soldiers would shoot arrows down from the wall? Don't you remember how Abimelek, the son of Jerub-Besheth, was killed? A woman dropped a large millstone on him from the wall. That's how he died in Thebez. So why did you go so close to the wall?' If the king asks you that, tell him, 'And your servant Uriah, the Hittite, is also dead.'"

The messenger started out for Jerusalem. When he arrived there, he told David everything Joab had sent him to say. The messenger said to David, "The men in the city were more powerful than we were. They came out to fight against us in the open. But we drove them back to the entrance of the city gate. Then those who were armed with bows shot arrows at us from the wall. Some of your special troops were killed. Your servant Uriah, the Hittite, is also dead."

David told the messenger, "Tell Joab, 'Don't get upset over what happened. Swords kill one person as well as another. So keep on attacking the city. Destroy it.' Tell that to Joab. It will cheer him up."

— 2 Samuel 11:19-25

David not only succeeded in murdering Uriah with Joab's help, but several other highly trained soldiers died along with him. Several wives lost their husbands. Several children lost their fathers. Parents lost their children—all because of a king who lacked self-control, and who found the perfect accomplice to his dirty mission in Joab.

This was premeditated murder and Joab did not hesitate to be a willing accessory.

Sadly, this incident revealed yet another character flaw of Joab. He was a man of low morals and values. Joab could have easily pushed back against the king's orders or even questioned the king on his intentions. Uriah wasn't just any grunt, he was among the very best under Joab's command. Even if Uriah had been an ordinary soldier or citizen, had Joab's conscience become completely seared that seeing to the murder of an innocent man was sport for him?

He was so overly concerned with his title and position that nothing else mattered. He just showed himself to be a morally corrupt leader not worthy of emulation in any sense. David the king had erred greatly by ordering the death of an innocent man to cover up his own sins. But Joab had the opportunity to put the brakes on that runaway train. Instead, he quickly agreed to set up the battlefield execution. The onus of being compliant and not questioning such heinous and immoral orders lay with Joab.

Being a highly skilled and competent leader is great, but not enough. Being a leader with good morals and character is more important. The bottom line: A leader's gifts, talents, skills, et al. are only as powerful as the character that contain it.

Proverbs 22:1 explains it this way:

If you have to choose between a good reputation and great wealth, choose a good reputation.

ESSENTIAL LESSON

A leader will benefit greatly from identifying his or her values, and setting strong boundaries around those values very early on. So when faced with temptation, or asked to do anything contrary to those values, the answer remains the same: NO! Why? You already have a made-up mind concerning certain issues. That kind of resolve will help you not to give in to temptation or commit crime.

CHAPTER 10

NOT TOO LONG AFTER Uriah's death, David brought Bathsheba to his palace and made her one of his wives. She did give birth to a son. But the Bible says, "the LORD wasn't pleased with what David had done."

The king who was supposed to lead by morale example had just outrightly violated several of the covenant terms between the Israelites and their God. Most notably the 6th and 7th commandments, which clearly state:

> Do not murder.
> Do not commit adultery.
>   — Exodus 20:13-14

The laws were created so the Israelities would have a set of principles that would help them properly govern and give order to their lives. The terms of the covenant were set to maintain reverence and peace in their society, and to ensure that the Israelites were a model nation to neighbouring nations. A nation of high moral values.

Now the one who was anointed as king directly by God over them, who was to lead the way in showing the people how to live right, had just violated those very laws. And of course, once the laws are violated, several negative inherent consequences are unleashed.

God used the prophet Nathan in 2 Samuel 12 to confront David about his sins and coming judgment.

A summary of the judgment was as follows:

"You are the man! The LORD, *the God of Israel, says, 'I anointed you king over Israel. I saved you from Saul. I gave you everything that belonged to your master Saul. I even put his wives into your arms. I made you king over all the people of Israel and Judah. And if all of that had not been enough for you, I would have given you even more. Why did you turn your back on what I told you to do? You did what is evil in my sight. You made sure that Uriah, the Hittite, would be killed in battle. You took his wife to be your own. You let the men of Ammon kill him with their swords. So time after time members of your own royal house will be killed with swords. That's because you turned your back on me. You took the wife of Uriah, the Hittite, to be your own.'*

"The LORD *also says, 'I am going to bring trouble on you. It will come from your own family. I will take your wives away. Your own eyes will see it. I will give your wives to a man who is close to you. He will sleep with them in the middle of the day. You committed your sins in secret. But I will make sure that the man commits his sin in the middle of the day. Everyone in Israel will see it.'"*

Then David said to Nathan, "I have sinned against the LORD.*"*

Nathan replied, "The LORD *has taken away your sin. You aren't going to die. But you have dared to show great disrespect for the* LORD. *So the son who has been born to you will die."*

— 2 Samuel 12:7-14

Sure enough, Bathsheba's infant son fell ill shortly after birth and died. David comforted his new wife the best way he knew how. He slept with her, she conceived again and gave birth to another son. They named him Solomon.

Over the two years while David was dealing with his own personal issues back in Jerusalem, Joab and the army were out at war. Joab was about to capture the last standing city of the Ammonites—Rabbah—the highly fortified capital city of the kingdom of Ammon. He sent a message to King David, informing him of what he was about to do. He asked his king to come down so he could take the full credit for all of the work that Joab had done.

> *He sent messengers to David. He told them to say, "I have fought against Rabbah. I've taken control of its water supply. So bring the rest of the troops together. Surround the city and get ready to attack it. Then capture it. If you don't, I'll capture it myself. Then it will be named after me."*
>
> *So David brought together the whole army and went to Rabbah. He attacked it and captured it. David took the gold crown off the head of the king of Ammon. Then the crown was placed on David's head. The crown weighed 75 pounds. It had jewels in it. David took a huge amount of goods from the city.*
> *— 2 Samuel 12:27-30*

Joab really was any leader's dream second-in-command. His loyalty and devotion to his master were without question.

One has to wonder why Joab was trying so very hard to please this master of his. First helping him to murder Uriah, and now letting him claim all of the credit for his own hard work. One can't help but assume that after the incident with Abner, the relationship between the two wasn't exactly rosy, so this was another way of trying to get back into the good graces of his master. He really was seeking his complete acceptance and love.

David took command, finished off the city and took credit exactly as Joab asked. An outsider looking in would have thought: "Wow! What a super king!"

ESSENTIAL LESSON

Our actions matter and have consequences—as we saw in the judgment passed against David. As a result, we ought to be careful in all we do. Sadly, David sacrificed a few moments of pleasure for decades of pain for him and his family. Everything outlined in the judgment came to pass in his life. We should learn from the mistakes of others so we do not make those same mistakes.

CHAPTER 11

YEARS WENT BY AND Joab dutifully continued to carry out his duty as army general. David had settled into his role as king over all of Israel. His sons, the royal princes, had grown up to become fine young men. They worked closely with their father on kingdom affairs.

It happened that Amnon, David's first son and heir apparent to the throne, had fallen in love (more like lust) with his very beautiful half-sister Tamar. Absalom, David's third son, was Tamar's brother by the same mother.

Amnon really wanted to sleep with Tamar. He wanted to so badly that he made himself physically ill just from the thought. With the help of his cunning cousin and adviser Jonadab, he hatched up a crafty plan that caused Tamar to walk into their trap. Amnon then raped her. After Amnon had his way with Tamar, he had her forcefully thrown out of his house like a piece of trash. Tamar had been defiled by her own brother. She ended up spending the rest of her life living in Absalom's house.

David of course heard about the assault.

King David heard about everything that had happened. So he became very angry. And Absalom never said a word of any kind to Amnon. He hated Amnon because he had brought shame on his sister Tamar.

— 2 Samuel 13:21-22

David, though angry at what Amnon had done, did not confront him, nor did he punish him for what he did to Tamar. David loved his children, but sadly indulged them.

Two years after the rape, Absalom organized an event out of town at Baal Hazor. He invited his father David and all of his brothers, including the despised Amnon, to this feast. David decided not to go, but gave Absalom his blessing. Amnon and the other princes went to the banquet.

Absalom ordered his men to kill his brother Amnon at the banquet, as revenge for raping Tamar. After all, his father did not do anything about the incident, so Absalom took matters into his own hands. Absalom fled to Geshur afterward, and took refuge there with his grandfather, Talmai. Macaah, Absalom's mother, was the daughter of Talmai, king of Geshur. Absalom stayed in Geshur for three years.

ESSENTIAL LESSON

A leader must do what is needed even when difficult and uncomfortable. This is part of leadership. It comes with the territory. Confrontations or even reprimanding for bad behavior—even as serious as murder and rape—seemed to be two things David did not like to do. When Joab murdered Abner, David took no action. We saw his inaction again in the case of Amnon's rape of Tamar. Confronting and reprimanding for bad behavior may be very uncomfortable for you, but they are necessary and should be carried out when needed, and in a timely fashion. Issues do not just disappear because they are ignored. Instead they fester. If David had at least rebuked Amnon for his abhorrent behavior it would have set a great example and precedence for his other children, not to mention his kingdom. It also may have prevented Absalom's later slaying of Amnon. If David had disciplined Joab for murdering Abner, he could have helped to instill some very valuable lessons about leadership in him, and perhaps prevented him from doing such again in the future.

CHAPTER **12**

IN THE THIRD YEAR after Absalom murdered his brother, the king's grief over the loss of his son Amnon had subsided, and he also really missed Absalom and longed to see him.

However, Absalom had committed capital murder, and according to Jewish law the penalty was death. *"Anyone who kills another human being must be put to death,"* says Leviticus 24:17. And Exodus 21:12-14: *Anyone who hits and kills someone else must be put to death. . . . But suppose they kill someone on purpose. Then take them away from my altar and put them to death:"*

Well this was quite a conundrum because David at this point had already lost two sons—the baby that Bathsheba bore from their adulterous relationship, and Amnon the slain heir apparent. No parent in their right mind would give the go ahead to have his or her child murdered, no matter the crime. Also, Absalom was now under the protection and jurisdiction of his grandfather, the King of Geshur. Going to Geshur to ask for the extradition of Absalom, would be instigating a war that I'm sure neither kingdom wanted.

Lastly, if King David pardoned Absalom, he risked being viewed as weak and partial. Any of his constituents who committed murder could easily say the king had no right to execute justice, since he pardoned his own son for the same sin. It truly was quite a conundrum.

Joab, being the shrewd political strategist and diplomat that he was, knew all about the ramifications of the crime Absalom had committed. He came up with a solid plan that would help bring Absalom back into Jerusalem while protecting the integrity of the king at the same time:

Joab got a woman from Tekoa. Tekoa is known for its olive oil. Olive oil is synonymous with wisdom in the Bible. This woman was known as the "Wise woman from Tekoa."

Joab took it upon himself to coach the woman on what to say and do before King David.

The woman from Tekoa went to the king. She bowed down with her face toward the ground. She did it to show him respect. She said, "Your Majesty, please help me!"

The king asked her, "What's bothering you?"

She said, "I'm a widow. My husband is dead. I had two sons. They got into a fight with each other in a field. No one was there to separate them. One of my sons struck down the other one and killed him. Now my whole family group has risen up against me. They say, 'Hand over the one who struck down his brother. Then we can put him to death for killing his brother. That will also get rid of the one who will receive the family property.' They want to kill the only living son I have left, just as someone would put out a burning coal. That would leave my husband without any son on the face of the earth to carry on the family name."

The king said to the woman, "Go home. I'll give an order to make sure you are taken care of."

But the woman from Tekoa said to him, "You are my king and master. Please pardon me and my family. You and your royal family won't be guilty of doing anything wrong."

The king replied, "If people give you any trouble, bring them to me. They won't bother you again."

She said, "Please pray to the LORD your God. Pray that he will keep our nearest male relative from killing my other son. Then my son won't be destroyed."

"You can be sure that the LORD lives," the king said. "And you can be just as sure that not one hair of your son's head will fall to the ground."

Then the woman said, "King David, please let me say something else to you."

"Go ahead," he replied.

The woman said, "You are the king. So why have you done something that brings so much harm on God's people? When you do that, you hand down a sentence against yourself. You won't let the son you drove away come back. All of us must die. We are like water spilled on the ground. It can't be put back into the jar. But that is not what God desires. Instead, he finds a way to bring back anyone who was driven away from him.

"King David, I've come here to say this to you now. I've done it because people have made me afraid. I thought, 'I'll go and speak to the king. Perhaps he'll do what I'm asking. A man is trying to separate me and my son from the property God gave us. Perhaps the king will agree to save me from that man.'

"So now I'm saying, 'May what you have told me prevent that man from doing what he wants. You are like an angel of God. You know what is good and what is evil. May the LORD your God be with you.'"

Then the king said to the woman, "I'm going to ask you a question. I want you to tell me the truth."

"Please ask me anything you want to," the woman said.

The king asked, "Joab told you to say all of this, didn't he?"

The woman answered, "What you have told me is exactly right. And that's just as sure as you are alive. It's true that Joab directed me to do this. He told me everything he wanted me to say. He did it to change the way things now are. You are as wise as an angel of God. You know everything that happens in the land."

Later the king said to Joab, "All right. I'll do what you want. Go. Bring back the young man Absalom."

Joab bowed down with his face toward the ground. He did it to honor the king. And he asked God to bless the king. He said, "You are my king and master. Today I know that you are pleased with me. You have given me what I asked for."

Then Joab went to Geshur. He brought Absalom back to Jerusalem. But the king said, "He must go to his own house. I don't want him to come and see me." So Absalom went to his own house. He didn't go to see the king.

— 2 Samuel 14:4-24

So Absalom returned to Jerusalem and was put under house arrest of sorts. For two years he did not see his father—the king. For two years he was deprived of all of the many privileges and benefits that came with being the king's son—a prince. Not to mention the supposed heir apparent to the throne. For two years Absalom lived like every other common citizen of the land. This was a slap on the wrist for his heinous crime. But to Absalom it felt like life imprisonment. After all, the reason he murdered his older brother in cold blood was because his father had not acted. Absalom had even waited two years before taking matters into his own hands. So he felt that he could not really be blamed.

Absalom decided to do something about his exile within the kingdom. Well, guess to whom he reached out, to help him get his rights and privileges restored? Joab! After all, he was the one who arranged to have him back in Jerusalem. He also knew that Joab had the king's ear always. He was his father's right-hand man.

But, as it turns out, Joab at this point was not exactly fond of Absalom.

ESSENTIAL LESSON

Choose to be a problem-solver—not one among the masses who only complains about the problem. Add value to others or your organization by being a problem-solver. Joab was adept at coming up with solutions to problems, but his problem was his solutions were not always the best. However, when faced with a pressing problem, Joab was never one to fold his hands and sit back, waiting for someone else to solve it. He took direct action. This was just one of the many traits that made Joab invaluable to David and the Kingdom of Israel. It is so easy to talk about problems we face. Anyone can do that! But it takes a lot of bravado and a special kind of person to attempt to solve the problem. All of David's officials saw the fix that the king was in regarding Absalom. None of them did anything. Joab did, without even being asked. For all of his flaws, Joab did his job well. He exceeded expectations many times.

CHAPTER 13

WELL, JOAB REFUSED TO go see Absalom. Absalom sent for him twice, and was rebuffed each time. Joab was sending a very clear and strong message: He had not helped get Absalom back into Jerusalem because he had a soft spot for him. He had done so mostly for his own personal gain.

Joab may have become tired of seeing David pining for his beloved son day in and day out, but this shrewd strategist also saw the situation as the perfect opportunity to accumulate more "brownie points" for himself. He no doubt thought that the more points he gained from his boss, the more secure his much-loved position and prestige were.

The third time Absalom sent for Joab, which Joab again refused, Absalom ordered his servants to set Joab's barley field on fire. That got Joab's attention very fast. So Joab went to see Absalom, and asked why he set his field on fire. Absalom claimed he had no other choice. He reminded Joab that he had reached out to him several times, with no results.

At Absalom's request, Joab agreed to talk to the king on Absalom's behalf. King David listened to Joab and agreed to see Absalom:

Then the king sent for Absalom. He came in and bowed down to the king with his face toward the ground. And the king kissed Absalom.

— 2 Samuel 14:33

So the king kissed and made up with his delinquent son. All was fine—or so they thought.

It wasn't long after Absalom was reinstated that he embarked on a mission to turn the hearts of the people of Israel away from his father toward him. Here is how he did it:

Some time later, Absalom got a chariot and horses for himself. He also got 50 men to run in front of him. He would get up early. He would stand by the side of the road that led to the city gate. Sometimes a person would come with a case for the king to decide. Then Absalom would call out to him, "What town are you from?" He would answer, "I'm from one of the tribes of Israel." Absalom would say, "Look, your claims are based on the law. So you have every right to make them. But the king doesn't have anyone here who can listen to your case." Absalom would continue, "I wish I were appointed judge in the land! Then anyone who has a case or a claim could come to me. I would make sure they are treated fairly."

Sometimes people would approach Absalom and bow down to him. Then he would reach out his hand. He would take hold of them and kiss them. Absalom did that to all the Israelites who came to the king with their cases or claims. That's why the hearts of the people were turned toward him.

— 2 Samuel 15:1-4

Absalom was not only very cunning and crafty, He was indeed a sight to behold! He was charming and extremely handsome. He was very much aware of his good looks, and the whole of Israel knew it, too. It is said of Absalom that not one single blemish could be found on him. Plus he had "locks of the gods"—long flowing hair. All of this made him very appealing to the people.

> *"In all Israel there was not a man so highly praised for his handsome appearance as Absalom. From the top of his head to the sole of his foot there was no blemish in him."*
>
> *— 2 Samuel 14:25*

Besides his considerable charms, Absalom also had authority and influence—being the son of the king and the heir apparent. Yes, he had all of the makings of a great leader—but only on the outside.

Absalom was a prince who had gone rogue!

ESSENTIAL LESSON

Trust should always be proven over time and not quickly bestowed, especially in a situation where trust has previously been broken or violated. After Absalom was pardoned and reinstated as prince, the king should have put him on a probation of sorts, with a trusted official watching his every move to ensure he truly was a changed person. The king was once again tragically blinded by his love for his son. King David's failure to apply these cautionary measures allowed the rogue prince Absalom to go behind his back, gain the hearts of so many people and undermine his father's authority.

CHAPTER 14

WITH THE GOOD LOOKS, long hair and charming personality, it is easy to see how the rebel prince charming was able to deftly undermine his father's authority, and become widely loved and adored throughout Israel.

I still wonder how his father or even Joab did not catch wind of what Absalom was doing. They must have really underestimated him or thought he had learned from his mistakes and turned a new leaf.

Four years after being reinstated as prince, Absalom lied to his father that he had to go to Hebron to redeem a vow he made to God while he was in exile. David quickly granted him permission and his blessings. At Hebron, Absalom put the finishing touches on the coup d'etat he had long been planning.

A messenger was able to warn David about what Absalom had done. The king and all of those surrounding him were in grave danger. It was only a matter of time before Absalom and his henchmen returned to Israel to lay claim to the throne. He already had all of Israel on his side. This was one war that David could not fight to win. His own people had now been turned against him by his own son, of all people. The king had no choice but to run, and run he did—right away and in broad daylight. Had he not, he and everyone on his side in the city of Jerusalem would be killed.

David hastily fled town with loyal Joab by his side, along with his special troops, palace guards and family members. They left Jerusalem weeping, in shame. The king ousted by his own son, whom he had given a second chance.

David had made several allies during his reign among whom were kings and other men of great wealth and prominence. So they provided him with shelter and sustenance during his escape. In fact, it was his trusted friend Hushai the Arkite who stayed back in Jerusalem to try to counter the advice and counsel of Ahitophel, David's former chief counsel and adviser, who had switched his allegiance to Absalom.

News soon got to David that Absalom was preparing for war. He intended to hunt his father down to kill him and his loyal troops, to erase all doubt that Absalom was the new king of Israel. David quickly divided his troops into groups: He put one under the command of Abishai (Joab's brother), another under Joab, and the third group under Ittai, an outsider from Gittite, who nonetheless had insisted on following David, along with all of his men and their families. David himself initially planned to march out with the troops, but his men discouraged him from doing so because he was the prize that Absalom was after. David heeded their advice.

As his commanders led their soldiers out to fight against his own flesh and blood, David stood by the city gate and exhorted them: "Be gentle with the young man Absalom. Do it for me."

Even after all this dark-hearted, ungrateful son had done—not to mention now wanted to kill him—this king who had already experienced so much loss, could not bear to lose another son. You could clearly hear the heartfelt cry of a father here.

ESSENTIAL LESSON

To every action there is always a reaction. It is also worth noting that the consequences of our decisions not only affect us, but those around us—either for better or for worse. This sad episode of the king forced to flee his own kingdom is another reminder that there are repercussions to our actions. Vices especially carry severe consequences. That is why we should strive to always make wise choices. All of the events that unfolded in this chapter were part of the judgment God handed down to David for his vices. God forgave David, but the consequences of his actions remained. God will forgive us for our transgressions, but many times the ramifications of our choices remain and we have to live with them or be reminded of them for the rest of our lives.

CHAPTER **15**

THE BATTLE TOOK PLACE in the forest of Ephraim. It was fierce, intense and bloody. Over twenty thousand men died. During the battle, Absalom's mule went under a large oak tree with thick branches. Absalom's long hair became entangled in the branches.

Imagine a man who the Bible says cut his hair just once a year and weighed it. His cut hair weighed five pounds!

Now, you'd think anyone with that much hair would have tied it back in battle. Especially a battle in a forest. Not Absalom. His pride in his good looks and long hair got the better of him.

So now the prince who would be king was left dangling in the tree by his hair after his mule galloped away, leaving him in a very vulnerable position. The Bible does not say why Absalom was alone when this happened, as someone of his status usually had armor-bearers and guards constantly nearby.

But it does say what happened next:

One of David's men saw what had happened. He told Joab, "I just saw Absalom hanging in an oak tree."

Joab said to the man, "What! You saw him? Why didn't you strike him down right there? Then I would have had to give you four ounces of silver and a soldier's belt."

But the man replied, "I wouldn't do anything to hurt the king's son. I wouldn't do it even for 25 pounds of silver. We heard the king's command to you and Abishai and Ittai. He said, 'Be careful not to hurt the young man Absalom. Do it for me.' Suppose I had put my life in danger by killing him. The king would have found out about it. Nothing is hidden from him. And you wouldn't have stood up for me."

Joab said, "I'm not going to waste any more time on you." So he got three javelins. Then he went over and plunged them into Absalom's heart. He did it while Absalom was still hanging there alive in the oak tree.

— 2 Samuel 18:10-14

The men surrounding Joab, carrying his armor, finished the job by further striking Absalom to ensure he was truly dead.

Joab's men then threw Absalom's body into a deep pit in the forest. The battle was over, David's men had won and the man after him was dead. Joab had just carried out yet another cold-blooded killing—this time the king's son.

The passage: "Suppose I had put my life in danger by killing him. The king would have found out about it. Nothing is hidden from him. **And you wouldn't have stood up for me**," speaks volumes about what the men under Joab thought of him, and sadly about the type of man Joab was. Without a second thought, he would very quickly throw a friend, ally or one of his own men under the bus just to protect his own selfish interests. What a despicable leader!

Did Absalom the rebel prince deserve to die? Yes. If he had gotten to his father first, he would have killed him. However, Joab outrightly went against his master's command. Here we see another effect of the dysfunctional relationship of Joab and David play itself out. David had become overly reliant on his army commander. Joab was most often out on the battlefield fighting wars that David should have been fighting. As a result, Joab often acted like he had carte blanche to act as he thought best. In this case, even ignoring his king's direct command to spare Absalom. After all, he was the one out on the field yet again. Having a highly competent army general was no excuse for David to become slack and complacent in carrying out his duties. The tragic consequence this time: another son was dead.

Ahimaaz, son of Israel's high priest and friend of David, asked Joab if he could run ahead of everyone else to go deliver what he thought was great news to the king, that Absalom, who revolted against him, was dead. Joab knew David would not take the news well. So Joab instead selected a Cushite—a foreigner, someone not from the king's inner circle to do so. Joab hoped that might somehow lessen the blow somewhat.

But Ahimaaz insisted and took off. He was a swift runner, so he outran the Cushite and reached David first. On getting to the king, he saw that the king was anxious. Not so much about the war, but about Absalom's wellbeing. Was he alive or dead? Those were the questions that had remained on David's mind from the moment his men went off to war against his rebellious son. When he spotted Ahimaaz, he thought, "Surely he brings good news. Ahimaaz is my buddy." Upon reaching David, Ahimaaz quickly had a change of heart about giving the king an upsetting report.

The king [immediately] asked, "Is the young man Absalom safe?"
Ahimaaz answered, "I saw total disorder. I saw it just as Joab was about to send the king's servant and me to you. But I don't know what it was all about."
— 2 Samuel 18:29

Ahimaaz had to change his tune. By hedging his answer with "I saw total disorder," and implying he did not know what happened to Absalom. In other words, he was really saying, "I'm not going to be the one to give you news you do not want to hear."

But the bad news came soon enough.

The Cushite arrived a few minutes after Ahimaaz. He was asked about Absalom and he told David that Absalom had been killed in battle. The king's reaction was not what the Cushite expected. David broke down sobbing loudly.

> *The king was very upset. He went up to the room over the entrance of the gate and wept. As he went, he said, "My son Absalom! My son, my son Absalom! I wish I had died instead of you. Absalom! My son, my son!*
>
> — *2 Samuel 18:33*

When news got back to Joab that the king was deeply upset and in mourning, the troops and their commanders felt as though they had lost the battle. Their joy from winning immediately turned into deep sorrow. They quietly marched back into the city—not triumphantly, but like men who were ashamed as if they had run away from battle. This was not how they expected to be celebrating the great victory that they all had helped to bring about.

Joab was furious! Enough was enough. After all, it was David's failure as a parent that had led to all of this in the first place. If he did not suck as a parent, had not overindulged his sons, and had handled the situation properly when he initially heard that Amnon had raped Tamar, maybe they would have avoided all of this.

He marched right up into the house of the king and without mincing words said to him:

"Today you have made all your men feel ashamed. They have just saved your life. They have saved the lives of your sons and daughters. And they have saved the lives of your wives and concubines. You love those who hate you. You hate those who love you. The commanders and their troops don't mean anything to you. You made that very clear today. I can see that you would be pleased if Absalom were alive today and all of us were dead. Now go out there and cheer up your men. If you don't, you won't have any of them left with you by sunset. That will be worse for you than all the troubles you have ever had in your whole life. That's what I promise you in the LORD's name."

— 2 Samuel 19:5-7

David did not dare say a word back. He got right up and did as Joab commanded. The king took his seat at the entrance of the city gate. His men were told, "The king is sitting in the entrance of the gate." Then all of them came and stood in front of him.

ESSENTIAL LESSON

We all need a trusted confidant in our corner who will be bold enough to tell us the truth, even when it is the last thing we want to hear. By choosing to mourn over Absalom instead of welcoming and hailing his victorious soldiers, David could have lost their allegiance and support. The king, though blinded by sorrow at that moment, was wise enough to recognize the truth in all that Joab told him, and he was humble enough to obey his second in command—no questions asked.

Another key point is that Joab addressed the king in private. He did not capitalize on his vulnerability by dressing him down in front of the troops. This would have been humiliating for the bereaved king.

CHAPTER 16

SHORTLY AFTER ABSALOM'S DEATH, David made plans to return to Jerusalem and reclaim his position as king of Israel. It was very important that he did this very quickly. David was liked by many, but there were still a lot of people who would prefer that he was not their king. Furthermore, failure to return to his throne could result in another insurgent or uprising. Bottom line was that the throne could not be left empty for too long.

To get the ball rolling. David sent messages to two of the highest-ranking officials in Jerusalem–Zadok and Abiathar, the priests.

David said, "Speak to the elders of Judah. Tell them I said, 'News has reached me where I'm staying. People all over Israel are talking about bringing me back to my palace. Why should you be the last to do something about it? You are my relatives. You are my own flesh and blood. So why should you be the last to bring me back?' Say to Amasa, 'Aren't you my own flesh and blood? You will be the commander of my army for life in place of Joab. If that isn't true, may God punish me greatly.'"

*So the hearts of all the men of Judah were turned toward
David. All of them had the same purpose in mind. They sent a
message to the king. They said, "We want you to come back. We
want all your men to come back too." Then the king returned.*
— *2 Samuel 19:11-15*

As part of the negotiations David made to retake the throne,
he replaced Joab with Amasa—Absalom's former army general and
son of David's other step sister, Abigail, as his supreme commander.

Amasa's mother and Joab's mother were sisters, making Joab and
Amasa cousins.

It is worth mentioning that David must have done something
similar with Abner, when Abner approached him about helping him
to become king over the other territories of Israel. Joab again had been
used as a political pawn by his master when he had shown nothing
but total loyalty and commitment to David. He must have been
infuriated and enraged by this new change. I also suspect that the
demotion was a way of punishing Joab for killing Absalom. David
probably was completely fed up with Joab at this point.

Yet, we have no biblical record of Joab saying anything, instead
continuing to serve dutifully. But I'm sure this must have been
deeply upsetting and insulting to him. The army general of David's
rebel son who had revolted against his father and was on the hunt
to kill them all, had now been made commanding general in his
place? Really?

The king and his men moved back to Jerusalem and David
was reinstated as king over all the land. Not long afterward, yet
another troublemaker popped up: Sheba, the son of Bikri of the
House of Benjamin and a relative of Saul—King David's predeces-
sor. He was also a prominent figure in the nation of Israel. Sheba
was able to stir up division in the nation by blowing his trumpet
and proclaiming:

"We don't have any share in David's kingdom!
  Jesse's son is not our king!
  Men of Israel, every one of you go back home!"
                                                    — 2 Samuel 20

He succeeded. The men of greater Israel deserted David and followed Sheba, but the men of Judah stayed with their king. The nation was again divided. David was back to having control only over Judah—Israel's southern regions. Something had to be done fast, otherwise David faced the possibility of losing control over Judah also.

He gave a directive to his newly appointed top general, Amasa. "Send for the men of Judah. Tell them to come to me within three days. And be here yourself."

Amasa did not show up in the stipulated time. Now precious time was running out. The more time went by, the greater ground Sheba gained in his mission, and the more likely a total revolution by the entire nation seemed. David was not used to this type of tardiness. Joab always did his job well. He always delivered, and on time. David found himself yet again in another conundrum. He could not ask Joab to lead the troops because he was the one who removed him from his position. It would also be embarrassing for the king. But he had to act fast otherwise Sheba would succeed in taking the kingdom away from him completely.

So David asked Abishai (Joab's brother) to act as interim commander. He was to lead the army in hunting down Sheba. Joab also went out on this mission.

When Abishai and the soldiers arrived at Gibeon, on their way to confront Sheba, Amasa and the soldiers with him met up with them. Joab, fully dressed in military regalia, stepped forward as if to greet Amasa warmly. They were cousins, after all. While giving his cousin a warm embrace, Joab plunged a dagger he had concealed in his left hand into Amasa's stomach. Amasa's insides spilled to the ground and he died there, in agony. Joab left him in the middle of the road, writhing in his own blood and innards in much pain until he finally died. Amasa's body was dragged from the road where he was slain and dumped into a nearby field. Clothes were thrown over him.

Joab's mission had been accomplished. He had just eliminated his rival and that meant he had his much-beloved title of supreme army general of Israel position back. Joab carried on with chasing after Sheba as though nothing had happened. For him it was business as usual. Murdering his own flesh and blood just happened to be one of those things he had to do. Let's also not forget that Amasa had chosen to side with Absalom and in a sense had betrayed his uncle— the king and his cousin— Joab. Murdering him was probably Joab's way of paying him back and also a way of letting those under him know that they would meet the same fate if they even entertained the thought of betrayal. Joab was very callous indeed. Not only that, he was overly ambitious. The position and title mattered more than anything else. It is also worth noting that the first time Joab murdered a perceived threat—Abner in cold blood, he was not held accountable for his actions. As a result he was emboldened to move forward with eliminating another rival—Amasa. When accountability is missing, irresponsible and even abhorrent behavior is perpetuated.

Sheba was found hiding in a fortified city in Israel called Abel Beth Maakah. Joab and his men surrounded the city and began pounding on its walls with logs to bring it down. A wise woman came out to make a truce with Joab. She offered Sheba's head in exchange for a cease-fire. Joab agreed. She spoke to the leaders of the city. They reasoned along with her that it would be foolish to destroy an entire city because of one man. Sheba was decapitated, and his head was thrown over the city wall to Joab. Joab then pulled his men from the city. Each went to his home and Joab returned to the king in Jerusalem.

ESSENTIAL LESSON

Ambition is a great motivator for success. When it is properly used, we can accomplish much. However, misplaced or unchecked ambition can turn into a destructive force that causes a person to cut down anyone perceived as a threat or rival. That ardent desire for power and rank is what drove Joab to excel greatly on one level as supreme commander of Israel. Ironically, that same force and desire drove him over the edge, causing him to murder those he saw as threats. Too much ambition can corrupt your soul. Evaluate your ambitions regularly.

CHAPTER **17**

DAVID APPARENTLY ACCEPTED YET another evil deed by Joab without much question or reprimand. Perhaps because once again, Joab had efficiently taken care of a big vexation—eliminating the Sheba threat.

One day, David decided to take a census of all of the fighting men in Israel. It does not seem like much of a big deal until one realizes the premise behind the census. The Israelites were very much aware that they remained undefeated because their God had always helped them in battles. David and his great army had experienced success after success not because they were the very best of fighters but because they had divine assistance.

> *David knew that the Lord had made his position as king secure.*
> *He knew that the Lord had made him king over the whole nation*
> *of Israel. He knew that the Lord had greatly honored his kingdom.*
> *The Lord had done it because the Israelites were his people.*
> — *1 Chronicles 14:2*

Under David's rule, the Israelites obeyed God and followed the terms of the covenant. They had a king who walked closely with God and is described as a man after God's own heart. David was far from perfect, but he strived to do God's will.

The fighting men were different from the soldiers. Fighting men were those of military age who could be called upon at any time to defend the kingdom.

Well, David had somehow forgotten that God was the real reason they were undefeated, and decided to take a census of all of the fighting men to see how truly powerful he was based on their number in his kingdom. He asked Joab to lead the project along with the commanding officers. Joab immediately saw the motive behind the census. He knew his master better than anyone else. Joab had been with him for just as long as he had been king. He knew this act would displease God. He tried to dissuade the king.

He said, "King David, you are my master. May the LORD your God multiply the troops 100 times. And may you live to see it. But why would you want me to count the fighting men?"
— *2 Samuel 24:3*

The king was adamant. It is recorded that The king's word had more authority than the word of Joab and the army commanders. That was true in spite of what Joab had said. So they left the king and went out to count the fighting men of Israel.
— *2 Samuel 24:4*

Joab was not too pleased. The book of Chronicles says he was disgusted with this command from the king. The assignment took him and the army commanders nine months and twenty days.

In Israel there were 800,000 men who were able to handle a sword. In Judah there were 500,000.
— *2 Samuel 24:9.*

David had once again displeased God greatly. Even David himself was convicted in his heart. He felt regret about ordering the census. He immediately confessed his sin to God and asked for forgiveness. But it was a tad bit too late. God again passed judgment, but then relented on personally harming David. But also once again, David's sin was very costly to those he ruled:

God sent a plague in which seventy thousand Israelites died, from Dan to Beersheba, in a single day.

∂∂⌒

ESSENTIAL LESSON

Followers of the God of the Bible choose to trust in a God who may not always answer all questions, or clearly provide all of the reasons why something happened. As "People of Faith," we believe he is all sovereign and always has our best interests at heart. An example is the one-day plague killing seventy thousand people, which is difficult to wrap one's mind around. Why did ordinary Israelites have to pay for the sin of one man, David? Perhaps there is more to the story than meets the eye. We do not know all of what transpired prior to David's census order. Bible exegesis does not claim to give a complete and exhaustive account of all events as written. Israel as a nation may have committed other sins not mentioned. The king's request for a census may just have been the tipping point that led to a judgment that affected so many, yet still spared the nation as a whole.

CHAPTER 18

KING DAVID WAS NOW much older, and. his health was starting to fail him. He couldn't keep warm even when blankets were spread over him.

So his attendants spoke to him. They said, "You are our king and master. Please let us try to find a young virgin to serve you. She can take care of you. She can lie down beside you to keep you warm."

So David's attendants looked all over Israel for a beautiful young woman. They found Abishag. She was from the town of Shunem. They brought her to the king. The woman was very beautiful. She took care of the king and served him. But the king didn't have sex with her.

— 1 Kings 1:2-4

The issue of royal succession soon became paramount. David's son Adonijah had become heir apparent to the throne, now that Absalom was dead. But God had told David that Solomon, whom Bathsheba had borne to him after the passing of the child they conceived in sin, would be king after him.

So David had announced to all of his officials and the entire nation that Solomon would be their next king:

David asked all the officials of Israel to come together at Jerusalem. He sent for the officers who were over the tribes. He sent for the commanders of the military groups who served the king. He sent for the commanders of thousands of men and commanders of hundreds. He sent for the officials who were in charge of all the royal property and livestock. They belonged to the king and his sons. He sent for the palace officials and the warriors. He also sent for all the brave fighting men.

King David stood up. He said, "All of you Israelites, listen to me. . . . [The LORD] chose me from my whole family to be king over Israel forever. He chose Judah to lead the tribes. From the tribe of Judah he chose my family. From my father's sons he chose me. He was pleased to make me king over the whole nation of Israel. The LORD has given me many sons. From all of them he has chosen my son Solomon. He wants Solomon to sit on the throne of the LORD's kingdom. He wants him to rule over Israel.
— 1 Chronicles 28:1-5

Naturally, this did not sit well with Adonijah, elder brother to Solomon, so he rose up and decided to claim his birthright. He put on quite a show by getting chariots and horses ready and had men run in front of him. All of this took place while his father was still alive but on his deathbed.

The Bible says this about Adonijah:

His father had never tried to stop him from doing what he wanted to. His father had never asked him, "Why are you acting the way you do?" Adonijah was also very handsome.
— 1 Kings 1:6

Another over-indulged (and handsome) son gone rogue! He felt empowered to declare himself king, even after his father had announced to the nation that Solomon would be the next king of Israel.

Adonijah discussed his plans with two very senior officials: Joab (who still controlled the army) and Abiathar, an influential priest. Both surprisingly agreed to support and help Adonijah in his defiant quest. Up until then, Joab had been completely loyal to his king and master.

As soon as David heard about Adonijah's intentions, he quickly arranged a coronation for Solomon while he was still alive, and had him sit on the throne as the new ruler and king of Israel.

King David said, "Tell Zadok the priest and Nathan the prophet to come in. Also tell Benaiah, the son of Jehoiada, to come." So they came to the king. He said to them, "Take my officials with you. Have my son Solomon get on my own mule. Take him down to the Gihon spring. Have Zadok the priest and Nathan the prophet anoint him as king over Israel there. Blow a trumpet. Shout, 'May King Solomon live a long time!' Then come back up to the city with him. Have him sit on my throne. He will rule in my place. I've appointed him ruler over Israel and Judah."
— 1 Kings 1:32-35

Once Solomon was officially crowned, that put an immediate end to Adonijah's plans. Now all of those who had agreed to help him were guilty of treason— punishable by death.

As David neared the time of his death, he gave Solomon specific instructions concerning Joab:

"You yourself know what Joab, the son of Zeruiah, did to me. You know that he killed Abner, the son of Ner, and Amasa, the son of Jether. They were the two commanders of Israel's armies. He killed them in a time of peace. It wasn't a time of

war. Joab spilled the blood of Abner and Amasa. With that blood he stained the belt around his waist. He also stained the sandals on his feet. You are wise. So I leave him in your hands. Just don't let him live to become an old man. Don't let him die peacefully."

— 1 Kings 2:5-6

In not so many words, David had ordered Solomon to ensure Joab suffered the same fate as those he murdered. Those were some of David's final words, and not too long afterward he died.

David joined the members of his family who had already died. He was buried in the City of David [Jerusalem]. He had ruled over Israel for 40 years. He ruled for seven years in Hebron. Then he ruled for 33 years in Jerusalem. So Solomon sat on the throne of his father David. His position as king was made secure.

— 1 Kings 2:10

He died when he was very old. He had enjoyed a long life. He had enjoyed wealth and honor.

— 1 Chronicles 29:28

Israel thrived under the rulership of King David. He had enjoyed victory after victory during his reign, helped greatly of course by Joab and by God's favor. The lowly shepherd boy became a powerful warrior, leader and eventually king over all of Israel.

ESSENTIAL LESSON

Perfection is not a requirement for great success. King David was a leader with many faults who faced a lot of trouble in his lifetime—much of it self-inflicted. He did not let that stop him from making a great impact with the platform he was given. He was an outstanding warrior and a great leader who for the most part lived to please God. Israel thrived and experienced many decades of peace and victory during his reign. In David we see a flawed leader who still went on to achieve great feats. He is credited with being one of the most popular kings of all time, and is revered in Israel to this day.

CHAPTER **19**

NOT TOO LONG AFTER David's death, Adonjiah went and spoke to Bathsheba, Solomon's mother. He asked her to speak to Solomon on his behalf and ask if he could marry Abishag, the Shunamite who helped to keep his father warm during his last days.

Bathsheba spoke to Solomon. Solomon, however, did not take kindly to Adonjiah's request. Abishag was privy to a lot of secrets and inside information, having been one of the few very close to David before he passed. Solomon saw the request as a direct threat to his position as king.

> *King Solomon answered his mother, "Why are you asking me to give Abishag, the Shunammite, to Adonijah? You might as well ask me to give him the whole kingdom! After all, he's my older brother. **And he doesn't want the kingdom only for himself. He also wants it for Abiathar the priest and for Joab, the son of Zeruiah.**"*
>
> *— 1 Kings 2:22*

Surely, Solomon always knew that his embittered older brother would not give up trying to become king. Adonijah had just provided Solomon with the perfect opportunity to eliminate a direct threat to his kingship—no matter that it was his own brother. He ordered Benaiah, head of the palace guard, to kill Adonijah.

Benaiah was one of David's top ranking, most-trusted officials and a brave and strong warrior. He was next in command after Joab, and commander of David's personal bodyguards. He carried out his new king's orders.

Joab soon heard that Adonijah had been executed. He knew right away that Solomon would waste no time in eliminating all those who posed a serious threat, especially Adonijah's leading conspirators—Joab being chief among them.

Joab knew right then that he was not going to live to see the dawn of the next day. Solomon was going to move swiftly. Time wasted meant giving the enemy time to plan a counterattack. Asking to marry Abishag in essence meant Adonijah still very much wanted to be king in place of Solomon. It also meant that he may have been acting on the advice of his co-conspirators. Joab was guilty on all accounts: guilty by association. There was no getting out of this wreck. After all, he was a seasoned and experienced political figure, he knew too well how situations like this ended. His fate was sealed.

Joab ran to the Lord's tent. The most sacred place, where the Israelities met with God. Joab, the powerful and mighty general of one of the greatest armies ever, now stared death in the face. Joab had served David faithfully for well over forty years. He was a master political strategist. He even stood by David when Absalom attempted to take the throne away forcefully. Now he faced certain death because he had miscalculated and had supported Adonijah. He was now considered a traitor—and about to face the final, full penalty.

Sure enough, Solomon gave the order to Benaiah. "Go strike Joab down." 1 Kings 2:29

This was no easy task for Benaiah. Joab was not only his boss but his brother in arms. He had fought alongside him in many battles. I am sure he even trained under Joab. They had worked side by side for probably most of Joab's many decades of service. It wasn't supposed to end this way. This time, Benaniah struggled with this order from the reigning king.

Benaiah entered the tent of the Lord. He said to Joab, "The king says, 'Come on out!'"

But Joab answered, "No. I'd rather die here."

Benaiah went and told the king what Joab had told him:

> Then the king commanded Benaiah, "Do what he says. Strike him down and bury him. Then I and my family line won't be held accountable for the blood Joab spilled. He killed people who weren't guilty of doing anything wrong. The LORD will pay him back for the blood he spilled. Joab attacked two men. He killed them with his sword. And my father David didn't even know anything about it. Joab killed Abner, the son of Ner. Abner was the commander of Israel's army. Joab also killed Amasa, the son of Jether. Amasa was the commander of Judah's army. Abner and Amasa were better men than Joab is. They were more honest than he is. May Joab and his children after him be held forever accountable for spilling the blood of Abner and Amasa. But may David and his children after him enjoy the LORD's peace and rest forever. May the LORD also give his peace to David's royal house and kingdom forever."
>
> So Benaiah went into the Lord's tent and stabbed him to death there, on sacred ground. Joab died and was buried in his home out in the country.
>
> — 1 Kings 2:31-34

In ancient times when a person died and was not given a proper burial, especially a person of high caliber like Joab, it was considered bad omen, almost like a taboo:

A man might have a hundred children. He might live a long time. . . . [but] suppose he isn't buried in the proper way. Then it doesn't matter how long he lives. . . . a baby that is born dead is better off than that man is.

— *Ecclesiastes 6:3*

This great man died like a commoner. His legacy as a great general alone could have lasted a long time. He could have been remembered more for his great exploits instead of his many misdeeds if only he had developed strength of character, held himself accountable and kept self-control.

ESSENTIAL LESSON

We sow today the harvest of tomorrow. This principle has held true and is still very relevant even now. Sadly, Joab's executions of those he saw as rivals and threats, sowed his own eventual execution because he was seen as a threat to the position of King Solomon. The legacy of this outstanding warrior leader is now marred forever by the actions he took because he let his insecurities and lack of self discipline get the better of him during his command and long career as army general and second in command to the mighty King David. The decisions we make today truly affect our tomorrow. Choose wisely.

EPILOGUE

THE STORIES AND EXPERIENCES in the Bible, especially stories of flawed men such as Joab, have been written, preserved and passed down through centuries so that we—- with our many flaws—might read them and be forewarned, inspired and even at times comforted, knowing that with all of our imperfections and flaws, we still can add value and leave an indelible mark in the world. But most importantly, these stories have been passed down from one generation to the next so that we can see and avoid the same pitfalls. By seeing the outcomes of the decisions the characters in these stories made, we can make resolute decisions not to repeat those mistakes and also learn from their mistakes.

The Bible verse below explains it succinctly.

God has breathed life into all Scripture. It is useful for teaching us what is true. It is useful for correcting our mistakes. It is useful for making our lives whole again. It is useful for training us to do what is right.

— 2 Timothy 3:16

The literal meaning of Joab's name is "My father is God." With his many talents and gifts, no one could doubt that. Joab truly was a gifted leader who surpassed every possible imagination and expectations of a commander of a great army. He excelled in leading his troops. He was a courageous and brave warrior. If we had been told that bravery was his middle name, no one would have doubted that for a second—because of the many victorious feats he accomplished. Joab was also a master political strategist who knew the political system of his time very well, and was able to use it to his advantage repeatedly. He was loyal to his master and king throughout his forty-plus year reign as army commander until the end when he fatefully agreed to support Adonijah.

On the battlefield, he was a beast! He never lost a battle. David even mentioned him and one of his exploits in the introduction to Psalm 60:

> *For the director of music. For teaching. A miktam of David when he fought against Aram Naharaim and Aram Zobah. That was when Joab returned and struck down 12,000 people from Edom in the Valley of Salt. To the tune of "The Lily of the Covenant."*

He showed such great competency on the battlefield that his master sent him off on his own to fight many of the battles that he should have taken the lead on. Sadly, that's where the good ends. Joab's many character flaws made one question if God truly was his father. His contemptible character did not reflect that of the God of the Israelites in any way.

Leadership did not change Joab, the higher platform only helped to magnify who he already was: an overly ambitious leader who did whatever it required to maintain his position and title. In the life story of Joab, we see a leader who lacked integrity and strong values. One who lacked self control and who manipulated situations for personal gain. From his life, we see that yes, it is great to be counted among the best and to be world class when it comes to how well one does his or her job. However, the values, morals and integrity of an individual matter more. Why? Because a leader's gift is only as powerful as the character that contains it.

The story of Joab is a great case study of what happens when a person finds himself or herself in a position of great leadership, but lacks the good character traits to bear the weight of such a position and the trappings of the role. Tragically, Joab with all of his gifts, talents and many achievements, did not finish well. Time and time again we saw in his life story how he reacted and responded when faced with situations that put a demand on his values and character. He failed miserably.

Our gifts and talents are given to us by God to serve humanity with. We benefit greatly when we use those gifts and talents to add value to others. To Joab, the title and rank mattered more than anything else. As far as Joab was concerned, his endowments were to profit him alone. Anyone seen as a threat was cut down. It did not matter even if the person was family—as in the case of his cousin Amasa.

Doing one's work well, with excellence, matters greatly and should not be ignored. However a person should work harder on character because it is a good character that guarantees the longevity of a leader's legacy. Joab's legacy is marred by his poor choices. Whenever Joab is mentioned, he will always be remembered not for his bravery and loyalty, but as being a miscreant.

As adults we are responsible for our choices and decisions; and we very well know the difference between right and wrong.

Long after God gave the initial 10 Commandments to the Israelites written on slabs of stone, those same laws are now written "on the hearts" of all of humankind:

"The days are coming," announces the LORD. "I will make a new covenant with the people of Israel. I will also make it with the people of Judah. It will not be like the covenant I made with their people of long ago. That was when I took them by the hand.

I led them out of Egypt. But they broke my covenant. They did it even though I was like a husband to them," announces the LORD. "This is the covenant I will make with Israel after that time," announces the LORD. **"I will put my law in their minds. I will write it on their hearts.** *I will be their God. And they will be my people. They will not need to teach their neighbor anymore. And they will not need to teach one another anymore. They will not need to say, 'Know the LORD.' That's because everyone will know me. From the least important of them to the most important, all of them will know me," announces the LORD. "I will forgive their evil ways. I will not remember their sins anymore."*

— *Jeremiah 31:31-34*

That is what helps every person to differentiate between wrong and right. The choice of freewill—to choose between right and wrong was given to all mankind thousands and thousands of years ago. When faced with the decision to choose between right and wrong, we should strive to always choose right, because the decisions we make affect us now and in the future. Those decisions define us and shape our legacy long after we are gone.

SUMMARY OF THE ESSENTIAL
LESSONS FROM THE STORY OF JOAB

- The path to seeing one's dreams accomplished is not linear. As a matter of fact, far from it. Just ask any successful person you know.
- When confronted with a choice of being brave or giving in to fear, choose to be brave.
- Every human being is endowed with a special talent: It is that thing that you do easily and better than most people.
- High risk often brings high rewards but, of course, the possibility of huge losses also.
- A lack of discernment—the ability to judge well, can lead to deadly consequences.
- A leader must do what is needed, even when difficult and uncomfortable. This is part of leadership. It comes with the territory.
- There is always more to the picture or story than meets the eye. Things aren't always what they seem. You should always be careful about jumping to hasty conclusions.
- Decisions you make when angry and emotionally charged, will nine times out of ten be decisions you regret. Whenever we make hasty decisions, we are bound to make mistakes.

- Be careful from whom you receive advice. Heeding to wrong advice from the wrong people can have devastating effects on you and those around you.
- A leader will benefit greatly from identifying his or her values, and setting strong boundaries around those values very early on.
- Our actions matter and have consequences.
- Choose to be a problem-solver—not one among the masses who only complains about the problem. Add value to others or your organization by finding solutions.
- Trust should always be proven over time and not quickly bestowed, especially in a situation where trust has previously been broken or violated.
- To every action there is always a reaction. It is also worth noting that the consequences of our decisions not only affect us, but those around us—either for better or for worse.
- Perfection is not a requirement for great success.
- Ambition is a great motivator for success. When it is properly used, we can accomplish much. However, misplaced or unchecked ambition can turn into a destructive force.
- Bible exegesis does not claim to give a complete and exhaustive account of all events as written.
- We sow today the harvest of tomorrow.

"A people who values its privileges above its principles soon loses both."

> — *Dwight D. Eisenhower,*
> *34th president of the United States*

ACKNOWLEDGEMENTS

A number of people have helped with the creation of this book, and for that I am so grateful. Before I thank anyone, I have to thank the Holy Spirit, who impressed it upon me to write this book. Joab has always been a character that I have been fascinated with for close to two decades now. There is not much written about him and for the most part he is largely eclipsed and overshadowed by his more famous boss – King David. Without the continued prompt from the Holy Spirit, even when many at times I wanted to say a flat-out NO!, this book would not have turned into a reality. I am glad I yielded to that prompt, as I have also learned a lot and grown as a person from the many lessons and principles discovered during the researching and writing of this book.

To my husband and Numero Uno – Wale, who has been tremendously supportive from the minute I told him I was going to write this book. It's one thing to yield to God's voice, but without your support and encouraging words, It is no exaggeration to say this book might not exist at all. I am so very thankful for your love, and continued support. For being my number one fan, and for your many great ideas. You are truly God's gift to me. You have believed in me every step of the way on this entrepreneurial journey, even when my ideas were outlandish. Your words of reassurance have allowed me to spread my wings and fly!

Caleb, Chloe and Isaiah. You make me so very proud. I am thankful God saw it fit to let me be your mom. Thank you for letting me write for hours on end on weekends with minimal disturbance.

I am grateful to my parents, I have benefitted from many years of support from them. My siblings, in-laws, aunts, uncles, cousins, too many to mention, you all rock! Thank you

Duayne Draffen, thank you for your contributions to this book and great editing skills. For taking the time to listen to my different ideas, suggestions and never-ending changes. You still let my voice shine through on every page as you transformed my writing.

Kimberly Martin, thank you for turning my vision for the cover and inside of this book into a reality.

And finally, to you, the reader. Thank you for taking the time to read my first book. I am greatly appreciative.

—November 2020

YOUR REVIEW MATTERS!

Did you gain any valuable lessons from reading this book? Kindly leave me a review on Amazon or anywhere else where you purchased this book. It makes a big difference to new and self-published authors like me. Every review counts. Thank you!

LET'S STAY IN TOUCH

Visit my website at www.yinkaadegbenle.com and be sure to join my mailing list. Upon joining, I will share my Top 10 Daily Affirmations with you. I say and pray these transforming affirmations regularly.

FOLLOW ME ON SOCIAL MEDIA

You can find me at:

LinkedIn: https://www.linkedin.com/in/yinkaadegbenle/
Instagram: @waysofexcellence
Facebook: @waysofexcellence

ABOUT THE AUTHOR

The characters of the Bible, especially those of the Old Testament, have always been interesting study subjects to Adeyinka. She enjoys spending innumerable hours getting to know them on an almost personal level via biblical accounts and other written works. Of greater importance from these stories are the many lessons and principles to be gained from their victories and missteps.

Adeyinka has built her platform of excellence coaching on the back of 20+ years of experience from Fortune 100 companies in the financial services sector, the non-profit industry and as an entrepreneur.

She strongly believes that excellence is the integral piece necessary for the success of an individual, organization and even a country at large. She teaches individuals and small businesses how to develop systems and habits of excellence that yield better results.

Adeyinka is a graduate of Long Island University, New York, with an MBA in International Business Relations. She holds a bachelor's degree from the University of Nottingham, United Kingdom. She is also a Certified Project Manager – PMI-PMP.

When she is not helping her clients, you will find her taking long hikes on nature trails. She is an avid lover and collector of houseplants (her "plant babies"), and she enjoys cooking and baking, especially for family and friends.

Adeyinka resides on Long Island, NY, with her husband and three children.

CPSIA information can be obtained
at www.ICGtesting.com
Printed in the USA
FSHW012335160121
77699FS